RAFFI

(Hakob Melik-Hagobian, c. 1835-1888)

JALALEDDIN

translated by

Donald Abcarian

Gomidas Institute
London

GOMIDAS INSTITUTE - ARMENIAN LITERATURE IN TRANSLATION

ABOUT THE TRANSLATOR

Donald Abcarian was born and raised in Fresno, California, where his family was part of the extensive Armenian-American community that has settled there since the turn of the last century. His earliest influences, including the Armenian language, derived from that milieu. He graduated from the University of California at Berkeley with a degree in philosophy and has pursued a lifelong interest in languages and world literature. His translations also include Raffi's *The Fool* and *The Golden Rooster*.

Published by the Gomidas Institute, 2021.

ISBN 978-1-909382-57-2

For further comments and inquiries please contact:

Gomidas Institute
42 Blythe Rd.
London, W14 0HA
Email: *info@gomidas.org*
Web: *www.gomidas.org*

INTRODUCTION

Jalaleddin is the first of Raffi's famous historical novels and was written in the immediate aftermath of the events it depicts.

On April 24, 1877, claiming to come to the defense of the long oppressed Christian subjects of the Ottoman Empire, Russia declared war on Ottoman Turkey. Within short order the Sheikh ul Islam (supreme Islamic authority) in Constantinople called for holy war. This amounted to a death warrant for the isolated Armenian and Assyrian populace of Aghpag, for it gave the green light to ambitious and restive Kurdish chieftains in the eastern provinces, among them Jalaleddin, to do as they wished with them. By mid-May, Sheikh Jalaleddin had received his marching orders from Constantinople and set out with his army to pass through Aghpag on his way north to join Ottoman forces in the strategic battle against the Russians at Bayazid.

Aghpag is the easternmost district of the province of Van [Vasbouragan], bordering to the east on Iran [Persia]. With its little mountain valleys and lush riparian plains, it sits astride the upper reaches of the Great Zab River. It's principal city is Bashkala (an ancient Jewish center, as well), and it is home to the ancient monastery of St. Bartholomew, known in Armenian tradition as the final resting place of the apostle Bartholomew. Its immediate neighbor to the east is the Persian province of Salmast, Raffi's birthplace, and it is clear that Aghpag always occupied a special place in his imagination. In one of his early travelogues, he describes his reaction on first stepping foot in Aghpag as follows: "Leaving Persia behind and for the first time setting foot in true Armenia it seemed I changed . . . ."

The Armenians of Aghpag were reputed as the most traditional of all Armenians, having kept their dress, their customs and their way of life unchanged from ancient times. During summer many of them assumed a pastoral life and went into the mountains with their herds to live in tents and move from place to place.

Their domestic life and social relations were said to be marked by a pristine simplicity and generosity and their robust youth impervious to the corrupting influences of the towns in which they worked. There they labored carrying heavy loads on their backs, but never gave a thought to forsaking their homeland as so many other Armenian youth were forced to do.

Jalaleddin's army entered Aghpag on May 14, 1877. Before the end of the month disturbing accounts of his exploits began filtering out and sent shock waves through the entire Armenian public. Correspondents' reports and eye-witness accounts received dramatic, sustained coverage in the Armenian press of the time, and Raffi himself spent long days and sleepless nights interviewing witnesses and survivors.

He was living in Akoulis and working as a school teacher when he finally completed the novel. His plan was to have it published the following May, 1878. However, due to certain mysteries in the transmission of the manuscript, Raffi received urgent notices from the publisher that it still had not been received by early May. Just a day or two before the scheduled publishing date the manuscript arrived at last and was published, as planned, on the exact anniversary of Jalaleddin's terrible invasion of Aghpag. It was received by the Armenian public with unprecedented acclaim.

Jalaleddin was first published as a separate book in 1884 and in ensuing decades was translated and published in literary collections in several languages: Russian, French, German, Bulgarian, Czech, Romanian and English (1906). The present translation is based on the text edited and annotated by Khachik Samvelyan in the Armenian language work Raffi: The Collected Works published by *Sovetakan Grogh* [Soviet Writer] in Yerevan, 1984.

Donald Abcarian
Berkeley, California
March, 2006

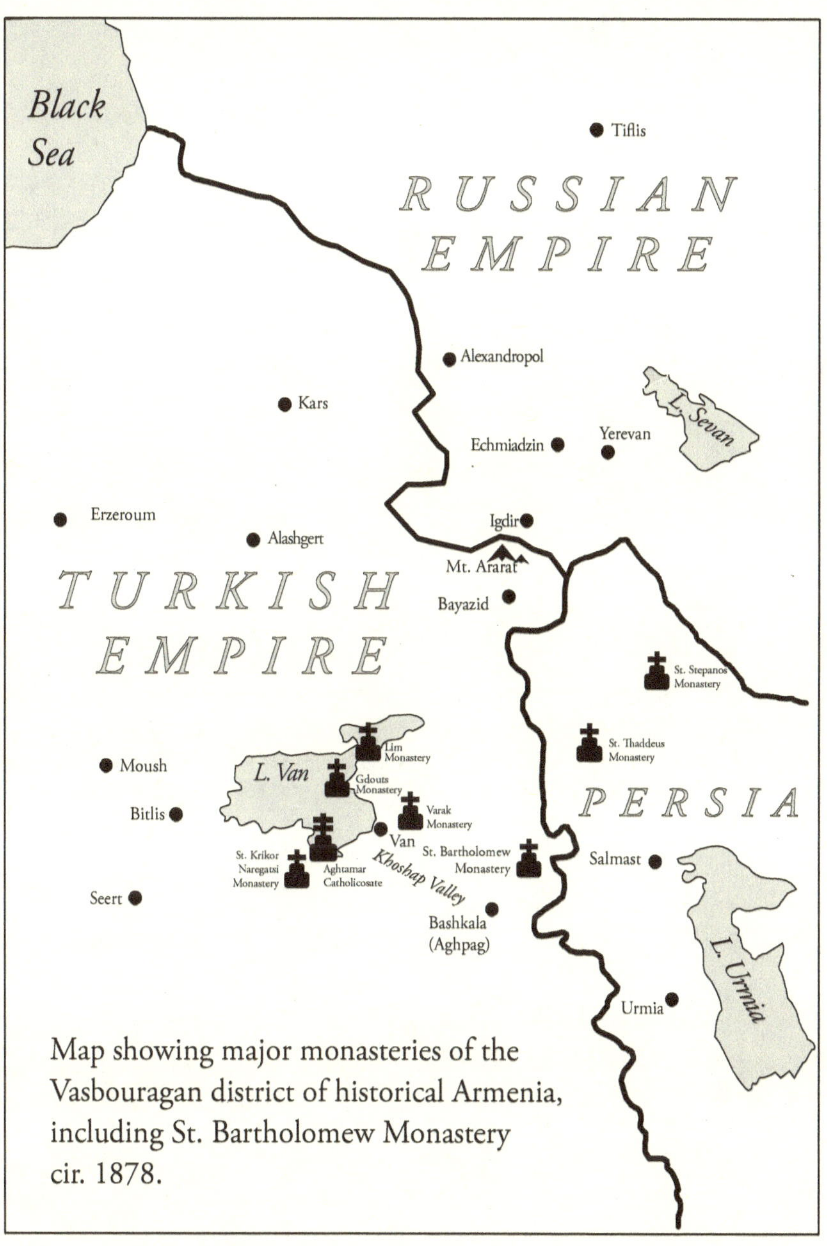

Map showing major monasteries of the Vasbouragan district of historical Armenia, including St. Bartholomew Monastery cir. 1878.

JALALEDDIN

CHAPTER 1

THE month of May 1877 was drawing to a close. In one of the fields of Aghbak's Liana Valley a number of black goat hair tents could barely be discerned through a morning mist. They were pitched close together and extended in a circle around a vast area set aside in their midst as an assembly ground.

It wasn't at all rare to see pastoral nomads grazing their animals in the lush pastures this valley offered, and at a casual glance one might have assumed these tents were theirs. But with the rising of the sun and the gradual thinning of the mountain mists an ever greater number of them came into view and the suspicious scene began more and more to reveal itself as a military encampment.

And, indeed, long cane-wood spears were stuck in the ground in front of all the tents. Their tips were decorated with black feathers. The assembly ground was filled with grim-faced fighters who were swarming about in a state of inexplicable excitement. Fully saddled horses stood grazing nearby in the tender grass, their legs fettered together.

One tent stood out from all the others by its size and majesty and in front of this tent was posted a red flag bearing four names in Arabic characters: Ali, Osman, Omar, and Abu-Bakr. In the midst of these venerated names of bygone Islamic Caliphs was the image of a white hand, the symbol of the invisible hand that would lead this armed multitude into battle. The tent was engulfed by a crowd and there was a continuous commotion as men went in and came out of it.

Inside, presiding over this rite from his seat on a thick felt cushion,[1] sat a man with flaming eyes and a tangled beard. He was of average stature and dressed from head to foot in white, attire that in the East is taken as an emblem of piety and signifies that its wearer, though still among the living, has already accepted the winding sheet of death. A long set of prayer beads,[2] divided into sections to keep account of the proper sequence and number of prayers, hung down from the right side of his broad belt; and on his left side, half hidden beneath the Aleppan cloak casually thrown over his shoulder, could be seen a curved dagger and the tips of two pistols. His head was wrapped in a white turban embroidered in gold thread with Arabic characters. He sat in the cross-legged position with a curved Damascene sword across his lap.

The esteemed old gentleman's outward appearance projected a persona in which religious fervor was wedded to the valorous spirit of war, for not only was he a high spiritual figure, he was also a mighty warrior. He was both sheikh[3] *and* general.

He presided as prince and patriarch from the highest and most honored position, flanked by rows of *aghas*[4] holding ancient weapons in their hands. Their intimacy with him was obvious and a sign that they weren't mere commoners but the leaders of the men who were gathered outside.

Next to the Sheikh sat a *kashkoul*[5] filled with triangular paper talismans. These resembled the talismans that sorcerers sometimes give to people for a variety of mystical purposes and they were inscribed with certain lines from the Koran that were supposed to protect one from harm in battle but which in reality possessed no magical power whatever.

The entrance to the tent was open and the men from the waiting throng went in and came back out one by one. Each began by kneeling and prostrating himself before the entrance, then proceeded to walk on his knees to the Sheikh inside. On reaching the Sheikh the entrant layed his sword at his feet and kissed his hand, whereupon the Sheikh took a talisman from the *kashkoul* and handed it to him. Then the man withdrew and exited the tent in the same manner as he had entered. Once outside, he wrapped the talisman in cloth and had it sewn into his right sleeve.

Thus with the continuous going and coming of the men the rite came to an end at last. Drums began beating outside and with that everyone in the camp came running from all quarters to converge on their exalted and holy commander's tent. When all were gathered there the Sheikh emerged and the entire crowd put their hands to their faces in a silent gesture of homage (*salavat*). This has the same importance to Muslims as crossing oneself has to Christians.

Because there was nothing else to serve for the purpose, the men piled all their saddles up to form a platform for the Sheikh in front of his tent. The Sheikh ascended the platform carrying the red flag of the Caliphate in his hand, not the staff traditionally held during sermons. This event hearkened back to that legendary moment in the middle of the desert when the prophet of Arabia[6] mounted a pile of saddles laid down by pilgrims to preach his first fiery sermon.

The Sheikh opened with fervent praises to Allah and elaborate blessings upon Mohammed and his main successors, Omar, Osman, and Abu-Bakr. He then continued in the following spirited manner:

"O children of Islam, the great prophet—praise be to his power—has called you here to carry out a great task; he's called on you to fight the enemies of his religion (and may they all be cursed!) who've drawn the blood of his followers. Banish all faint-heartedness and fear. Fear has no place in God's fighters. The Lord himself will give you power, and the enemy's necks will fall beneath your swords like straw beneath the sickle.

"You'll catch their shells in your hands and hurl them back. You'll be protected by invisible iron ramparts. The prophet will send the invisible hosts of destroying angels to fight beside you. Great is the God of Islam, and there is no other!

"All the *gavours*[7] are unclean in God's sight. Everything they own—their land, their life, their homes—all of it he commits to your hands. Ravage, steal and burn to your heart's content! God renders their blood and everything they own *halal*[8] to you. But he despises cowards, especially those whose hearts run cold and desert the battle. The enemy must never see your back! If you're fighting for God, then die with a sword in your hand!

"If you desert, God will drive your wife out of her mind, and you'll find her standing at the entrance to your tent when you go home, but not to welcome you. Instead, she'll shout, 'Go away! You're no husband of mine! Where are your wounds? Why did you come back alone? Where are your comrades? Get out of here! Any man who dishonors his weapons is no husband of mine.' A woman's anger is a terrible thing, but God's revulsion is worse.

"The Lord loves the flowing blood of the holy faith's enemies. He accepts as a sacrificial offering the smoke that rises to his throne from the ruins of their homes. Kill with all the strength you have! Set fire to everything! The more blood you spill, the greater the number of virgins you'll enjoy in Paradise!

"Great is the God of the true believers! There is no other!

"If you want to make concubines of the women you capture or take a boy as a servant, God doesn't forbid it so long as they accept Islam first.

But as for old people—women or men—show no mercy. Their resistance to our faith is as hardened in them as their brittle bones.

"Be fair in sharing your spoils. No one should be stingy with his comrades. And don't forget to set aside some of your spoils for God, because his angels have fought beside you on the battlefield. Show mercy to sick and wounded comrades, for beneath this holy banner you're all brothers."

The Sheikh went on at great length from his platform, standing there and exhorting his men as the very embodiment of the spirit of Islam, as the living exemplar of wanton cruelty and fanaticism. His voice was sharp and compelling, and his language wasn't devoid of a certain exciting eloquence. This would have been the only way for a follower of the Koran, in which holy war is extolled with such ravishing poetic power and bloody detail, to rouse a wild mass of men to slaughter their fellow human beings. To conclude his sermon he addressed his army as follows:

"God demands a vow of you and all of you must keep it."

At these words all the men picked rocks up from the ground and tossed them into one great pile thus forming a monument to their fearsome vow. And while this was going on the air resounded with thousands of voices within the roar of which the following words could clearly be heard: "And may our *talakh*[9] fall like these rocks if we break our vow." When all the rites were over the Sheikh repeated his blessings, descended the platform and disappeared into his tent.

The drums sounded again and all the fighters ran to mount their horses. The tents were taken down and within a short time the entire army was assembled and ready to go. With the red flag in his hand, the Sheikh mounted and led his army forward.

His sacrosanct visage was hidden beneath a white veil lest any infidel's gaze should fall on it. This forbidding old gentleman was followed by more than ten thousand Kurds. A line of camels piled high with small arms trailed along behind.

Thus began Sheikh Jalalledin's invasion of Turkish Armenia.

CHAPTER 2

ONE week later a young man was making his way along the road that leads from Van to Aghbak. Having left the Khoshap Valley only a short time before, he was already at the Choukha Gadik mountain pass. Nearly thirty years of age, with a clean-shaven face, sallow complexion, sunken cheeks and sharply jutting jaw, he was alone and on foot, pressing forward at an urgent pace. Snow-white teeth flashed through his ashen lips as they parted from time to time and his head of curly black hair rested on his bare, sunburnt neck. A deep scar on his brow added to the ferocity and forbidding cast of his expression, but there was also a certain virile beauty there — along with hints of valor, of daring, and of mad cruelty.

He was firmly built—tall, wiry and muscular—and dressed like a Kurd in full battle regalia, with an Asiatic rifle, a curved sword, a pair of pistols, a large iron shield on his back and a long spear, all of which he carried as if they were parts of his own body. As he went along he stopped from time to time to carefully examine the landscape around him. It wasn't the verdant beauty of the mountains that gave him pause, for he had no taste for beautiful things nor the inclination to be enraptured by nature. What struck him was that these familiar mountains were entirely deserted. Only ten days before he had come this way and it was an entirely different picture: the lovely mountains were covered with flocks of sheep grazing in rich pastures; the tents of the pastoral Armenians were pitched in the dales and from afar one could hear the sound of the sheperd's flute mingling with the morning song of the birds. That was the hour when the Armenian cultivator went about his work, singing his traditional song, planting or reaping in the valleys and mountain fields; the hour when man and nature were joined together in unceasing labor. But now . . . . ?

Now all motion had ceased. There wasn't even a single caravan on the road or any sign of people anywhere. It seemed some evil force had passed over the land to leave nothing but ruin and desolation in its wake.

The young traveler shuddered and his tanned face went pale—not out of fear, for he knew no fear—but because of an incredible fury that erupted deep inside him.

The road began rising in twists and turns toward the mountains. On reaching the summit he noticed the gleam of needle-sharp spears ahead of him down the road. Within a few minutes a group of horsemen came into view. They seemed to have caught sight of him as well and came to a halt as if waiting for him to catch up.

As he got closer the young man could see that the riders were Kurds, singing and celebrating like they do after a major victory. He knew the behavior of these half-civilized people so intimately that the smallest detail spoke volumes to him and so his heart started to pound when he noticed pieces of clothing suspended like flags from the tips of their spears. Any careful observer would immediately have recognized these as women's clothes; indeed, they were the undergarments that modesty dictated should never be seen by men. This was barbarism at its worst: fresh from violating the innocence of decent women and the chastity of young girls, these ruffians flagrantly displayed their undergarments as trophies of war, signalling their outrages against conscience and morality for all the world to see.

The young man checked his emotions and approached in a cordial manner, rendering the traditional Kurdish greeting:

"Happy traveling to you!"

"Happy traveling to you, too" answered the men.

"Where are you coming from?" one of them asked.

"From Van."

"Where are you headed? What are you up to?"

"I'm on my way to Bashkala[10] with a message from the Pasha to the *moudour*."[11]

The Kurds exchanged quizzical looks at his answer.

"And where are you headed?" the young man asked.

"The Sheikh called on us to fight against the *gavours,*" responded one of the men.

"I guess you tried your first luck against those paltry clothes," said the young man, pointing derisively at the clothes hanging from their spears.

"That was just some small game we came across on the way; our comrades burned an Armenian village and the women ran off . . ."

"Out of their hands right into yours, huh?" said the young man, interrupting the man's account.

"Where are you from, anyway?" asked one of the riders suspiciously.

"I'm a Heidaranli[12] from the Sipan[13] mountains," the young man answered in the Heidaran dialect.

"Aren't the Heidaranlis joining up?"

"Yes, but under their own Sheikh. The Shikags, Ravands and Bilbasts[14] will follow Sheikh Jalalledin."

This haughty statement from the Heidaranli didn't go over well with the riders, for they were Ravands. But seeing that he was a messenger on an official mission, they held their peace.

To change the subject the young man muttered as if talking to himself:

"What a horrible place! I've never been here before. There must be some shepherds or villages around. I'm dying of hunger and there's nothing to eat.

"There used to be people here—*Fuleens* [Armenians][15]—but a couple of days ago the Harkis[16] came through and laid waste to everything," said one of the men.

The dark look on the young man's face grew darker still and he struggled to maintain his cool:

"Were you left empty-handed, then?" he asked

"Well, there's plenty of game on the road to Bayazid. . . God is generous," the man responded.

"Goodbye . . ." said the young man as he made to leave and continue his journey. One of the Kurds took some cheese and bread out of his saddlebag and offered it to him.

"Have some. You said you were starving. It's a long way to Bashkala."

The young traveler took the food and thanked him. But as the band of outlaws rode off it suddenly became clear to him why he had been so disturbed just a few minutes earlier by the desolation of the landscape around him. Though he'd eaten nothing all day and was truly famished, he lost his appetite and threw away the food, for there are moments in life when a man makes a meal of the despair that fills his heart.

Chapter 3

THE sun was nearly set by the time our weary traveler reached a fork in the road. To the right was Bashkala and to the left the monastery of the Apostle Bartholomew; he took the latter road.

Never had there been a lovelier sunset. Never had the mountain air been lighter and fresher or the clouds more golden than on this evening, but our young sojourner felt nothing; there was no rapport between his inner being and the world around him. He continued on his way totally self-absorbed, impelled by some invisible force.

The air was still and quiet as darkness descended and the stars began twinkling gaily in the sky. This was the hour when great herds of sheep would be returning from their highland pastures and filling the mountains with the far off echoes of their bleating, a sound that evoked such precious images of pastoral life. Yet tonight there wasn't a sound. A deathly silence reigned everywhere.

Our young traveler had gone quite a way when through the gloom he began noticing little dots of fire at various points in the distance. They expanded and contracted alternately and at times shot up into the air like dragons. He stopped briefly to take in this frightful picture. For a moment, it occurred to him that the fires were chaff being burned off in the villages but soon dismissed this idea because he knew that it was too early for the grain harvest in these parts. He also knew that only Armenians inhabited the dales where the fires were burning.

He trudged on and so lost to the world was he that all these terrible scenes just passed before his eyes like a nightmare.

It was the middle of the night by the time he left the road and climbed a hill thickly covered with bushes. Reaching the top, he looked up at the sky for the first time and saw Drtad's Cross[17] standing at its zenith. Caught between hunger and fatigue he was completely exhausted and sat down on a rock to rest for a moment. From this vantage point he could see the dots of fire more clearly and he gazed at the heart-numbing sight.

Suddenly he caught the sound of hushed voices coming from the bottom of the hill:

"Good Lord, which way should we go . . . . . ."

"Let's just keep on going . . . We'll find someplace . . ."

"My knees are shaking . . . the baby is about to pass out . . ."

"Let me have him."

"Why are you falling behind, girl?"

"The stones are cutting my feet mommy."

The conversation stopped for several moments, then resumed:

"The fire is still burning . . . It's horrible!" said the wife

"Just watch out for the children . . . We're lucky to have escaped."

"But your head is starting to bleed again . . .You're wobbling . . . My God!"

"It's all right . . . the bandage just came loose . . ."

"Come here, let me tie it."

"No, we don't have the time. We have to get out of here."

The voices stopped again.

The fire in the nearby village flared up now and lit the bottom of the hill in a flash of light, revealing the tragic picture: a father was carrying a small child in his arms while his blood dripped down on the child's head and his wife was trudging along beside him leading their little daughter by the hand. The couple, totally exhausted, barely had the strength to continue on their way.

Darkness descended again, and once more the voices could be heard:

"Oh, what a massacre! . . . ."

"And they set fire to everything! . . ."

"Nothing's left . . ."

"Where shall we go now? Oh, God! . . ."

"I want something to eat, mommy . . ."

"Don't cry now . . ."

"Mommy!"

The voices ceased.

Our young traveler wasn't one to be saddened by catastrophe. Quite the contrary, it only made him angrier. He therefore looked down on the desperate flight of this family with nothing but diabolical coldness in his heart, and you could almost hear the following fateful words flying from his satanic lips :

"You deserve your suffering! You brought it on yourselves! Don't blame the burning and looting invaders."

This is hatred speaking in its most stupendous voice, springing as it does from love. It's the brotherly cry of warning to a brother unprepared to fend for himself in the struggle for existence. And from this hatred arises the sort of refined anger that pushes a man to the ultimate crisis point and transforms him into a forbidding messenger, one bound and determined to place a people's fate between two points only: either life or death. At such a moment he will say, "Anyone who's never understood, nor wished to understand, what life really requires has no right to live. And what life requires of a man at any given moment changes according to its shifting circumstances: when intellect is called for, he should be prepared to use his mind. But when it's time to use a sword he should have one ready in his hand, because human life is an arena of terrifying struggle. Those unable to hold their own will fall, will fade, will cease to be." But there was no such philosophical reasoning at the bottom of our young traveler's distress for he was a stranger to any philosophy of life. His grasp of human existence was based on the most obvious phenomena of nature and he had concluded that if the sheep is condemned to share the world with the wolf it should acquire the fangs of a wolf to avoid becoming its dinner, and circumstances had so ordained that against his will he had turned into that very wolf. He had been harassed at home as a child and forced out as a prodigal son. No one in his village cared for him. So submitting to his fate he became a wandering adventurer and ultimately turned into a heartless outlaw, one who vowed to avenge himself on mankind for the suffering he had endured.

But even as an outlaw he never totally lost touch with his decency and always maintained the leonine majesty that spares the weak or injured and leaves the greater part of the kill for smaller animals to feed on . . .

After ten long years away from his homeland he returned on hearing of the danger that threatened it. But it wasn't to save his homeland that he returned, for he well knew that even a great number of men like him would be powerless to accomplish that. No, he was helpless even to save himself. He returned to Aghbak to rescue his precious Asli, the only person in all the world that he loved and that returned his love; his only hope in a world that despised him and denied him a place to stop for a moment to rest, to breathe, to forget the bitterness of life.

This was what made him so callous about what was happening around him and impelled him forward without letup as if pursued by an evil spirit. But nature will demand its own. Having been on the road for several days on end without sleep, his energy was waning. When finally he reluctantly sat down on the hilltop to rest for a moment his head suddenly went heavy, his eyes closed, and he collapsed in the tender grass overwhelmed not so much by sleep as by a kind of tormented stupor.

Chapter 4

THE morning star had risen and the crimson line of daybreak had just begun to glow along the horizon when our young traveler suddenly roused himself and shuddered to discover that he had wasted the greater part of the night on the hilltop, time in which he could have gone a great distance on the road. He quickly grabbed his rifle and spear and set out on his way again.

When he reached the highlands of Aghbak he saw smoke rising from all the Armenian villages, an ominous smoke mixed with flames. He went into one of the villages and found its earthen cottages completely reduced to ash and gory corpses lying around grotesquely. For the first time he felt the full horror of what he had sensed the night before: those dots of fire which had so mystified him in the dark of night were all the burning Armenian villages of Aghbak.

This terrible scene might have struck another like a bolt of lightning, but not him, for it had always seemed to him that this is how things would turn out in the end; with his prophetic inner eye he had already glimpsed it in all its bloody detail. Having long since come to terms with his jeremiad, his heart was hardened and he had no tears left to shed for what he saw before him. It was therefore with a certain indifference that he surveyed this catastrophic scene where the bodies of slaughtered women, girls and children lay on top of each other, buried beneath the rubble of their own destroyed houses.

The human heart is truly remarkable: It sometimes seems an infinite space embracing whole universes while at other times like a completely filled vessel that won't admit anything new. And it is most remarkable of all when it is filled with love. But any new force seeks an empty place, while Sarhad's heart was far from empty. He had passed by village after village reduced to smoldering ruin, littered about with bloody, asphyxiated bodies, but all of this had only a passing effect on him.

Though the lowlands still lay in darkness the dawn grew brighter now and the sun's red-purple rays began to touch the snow-white clouds and give them a saffron hue. The young man continued on his unusual trajectory, pressing on toward the village of Yeresan, passing through rugged terrain which—with its stupendous ups and downs, with its narrow gorges and rocky precipices—was the mountain goat's exclusive domain. On reaching Yeresan he saw that here also fire and sword had put an end to everything—to people as well as dwellings. Here for a long while he searched among the corpses lying on the ground until he finally came to a halt in front of one particular cottage. It was still burning and he stood looking at it in deep silence.

This little cottage had been his home as a child. But where were his mother and father, his sisters and brothers now? They were no more. This terrible sight drew a few tears from his eyes and they ran down his sallow cheeks.

Tears are a remarkable manifestation of the inner feelings. There are tears of joy as well as of sadness. Yet more remarkable than these are the tears of anger. These were the tears our young traveler shed and they were mixed, like those that fall from the sky, with thunder and lightning.

There were some household objects lying near the cottage, evidently left behind by the invaders because they couldn't carry off any more. He recognized each one: his father's favorite rug, his own bed quilt, his mother's kneading bowl; the pan his sister had used to milk the sheep. Each object evoked old, old memories. He bent down and began picking them up; and one by one he flung them into the burning cottage as if to make the fire burn hotter.

Just at that moment two Kurdish riders appeared on the scene with some unmounted horses in tow.

"Why are you burning that stuff? We came back for it. We didn't have enough horses before, but now we do," said one of the men.

"There's still plenty left. Get down," the young man said coolly.

The Kurds dismounted and were about to collect the remainder of the goods.

"Stay back! I have to burn them!" the young man roared.

"Why?"

"I'll burn you too if you try to interfere."

"You?"

"Yes, me!" said the young man, and in a flash he brought his sword down on one of the Kurds and fired his pistol into the other's chest. He dragged their bodies to the fire and dropped them in, then grabbed one of their horses—the very finest one—and rode off.

After riding a while he dismounted and let the horse go, because a horse would have been useless to him on the steep and narrow paths he would take the rest of the way.

He had gone a good distance from his native village when he began to notice a dark spot far off in the highlands, quite prominent in the light of the rising sun. As he drew closer the object increased in size and seemed to loom in the air high above the ground. He pressed on toward it and the closer he got the more such objects he saw, objects that now began to look like scarecrows on poles. But far from having any power to frighten bird or beast, he saw crows and vultures and even the timid magpies flying around them quite happily, repeatedly flying off then circling back to perch on them again. Jackals and hyenas were making happy sounds and gathering around as if for a sumptuous feast.

The scene became clearer as he approached. He saw before him the worst horror produced in their ingenious cruelty by the Mohammedans. The forms impaled on the poles were human beings barbarously hoisted up while still alive, their heads twisted to one side. The horrified young man recognized their faces. They were two pastors and a *vartabed*[18] he had known. Other mutilated bodies lay on the ground around them, rendered still more grotesque by the fact that they had been fed upon by predators.

Suddenly a faint murmur struck the young man's ears, the awful sighing of someone in the grip of death. He hurried forward along a barely visible trail and noticed spots of blood on the ground. He had gone barely ten paces when he found an old man collapsed on the ground in front of him. The young man dropped to his knees and cradled his hoary head in his hands. A long silence ensued. The dying old man, not the vital youth, was the first to take heart and say something:

"O Lord, now take my soul. The son lost to me ten years ago is here to shut my eyes and I can die in his arms, at last."

The young man said nothing but sat with his head hanging down over his dying father. With the last of his dwindling strength the old man pushed his son's head up.

"Sarhad, incomparable Sarhad! Let me bless you, then I can die," he said.

"But first listen to my curse, then you can die," said Sarhad entirely beside himself. "Yes, you lost me ten years ago, but you forced me away from home. I wasn't a prodigal son, or an idler or drunkard. I just liked weapons and horses and hunting—innocent interests, but you hated them all. So you stuck me in a monastery to be an ascetic and spend all my time in prayer. When I ran away and came back home, you wanted me to work with a plough and a sickle and I did. But I didn't want to lay my rifle down because the Kurds were constantly plundering our crops. When it came time to defend ourselves you told me to be good and not answer evil with evil. You used to tell me, 'We're Armenians. We always have to keep our heads down and speak softly. We must never raise our hand against anyone.' That was what you preached to me. But I could see that the more I bowed my head, the more I was beaten; the more I bit my tongue, the more I was cursed. When I didn't lift a finger to protect myself, they took away the little I had and left me destitute and starving. You placed all your trust in God and told me to be patient. But after I saw how indifferent God was to all the evil we had to suffer I lost my faith. Your anger at me boiled over, and you kicked me out because I wouldn't follow our forefathers' example, because I hated servility and refused to lick our persecutors' feet . . ."

"But where did you go, what did you do after that?" his father asked.

"I became a wandering hunter. But it's only a short step from killing animals to killing human beings and I started robbing and killing people. And why not, when I saw that the men who did were better off than me and got more respect; when it was clear that good and decent people—people who'd never hurt a fly—had no control at all over their lives or property?" Sarhad paused for a moment to catch his breath, then went on:

"Don't you see, father? You were a good man, as meek as a lamb, but it didn't make any difference. And those priests impaled like scarecrows on poles, those corpses lying around them—I knew them all. They were all fine and decent men. But what good did that do them? They were cut down by evil just the same . . . No, evil has to be answered with evil, and goodness with goodness; that's what the injustice of mankind demands . . ."

"Stop torturing me, son! Let your poor father die in peace! Your tongue hurts more than any Kurdish spear!" the old man said, his voice trembling.

"No! If you haven't lived in peace, then you can't die in peace. Peace isn't for us—neither in our homes nor in the depths of our graves."

"Did you see our cottage?" his father asked.

"Yes. I saw it burning."

"And our family?"

"There was no one left. All I saw was dead people."

"Why couldn't you have hurried and got here a day or two sooner to save us?"

"I knew the invasion was coming, but I didn't come back to save you. What could I have done alone against such a horde? What could I have done for a people who sharpen their enemies' swords with their own hands? We're more to blame for the chains of our bondage than the invading barbarians . . . Those are the chains our forefathers forged and shackled their children with. So curses on them! They took every last bit of iron from our hands and didn't even leave us with a paring knife to use . . . They took away our heart and put a piece of dead meat in its place, all the while teaching us to be good, obedient, patient. Curses on them!"

Thus did Sarhad damn the sacred memory of his ancestors and hurl his fiendish oaths down upon his father's head, as if intent on stealing away the very last breath from the man who had given him the breath of life.

"Enough! Have you come here only to pour curses upon us?" said his father in a fading voice.

"No, our forefathers aren't even worthy of that. I came back for the woman I love. When my own family despised me and I was an outlaw who made hell tremble, she gave me her love. When I had committed crimes that horrified angels and devils alike, she still loved me. It was to save her that I came back."

His father dropped his head back down in Sarhad's arms without paying attention to what he had just said:

"You cursed us, but I bless you," he said, closing his eyes. His lips kept moving as he murmured a prayer that concluded, "O God, forgive my son."

These would be his last words.

Sarhad sat for a long time weeping over his father's lifeless body. This was the second time he had wept since returning to his native land.

At last he picked his father's body up and carried it to a gully. He used his dagger to carve out a hole in the soil and pressed his father's body into it, then covered it up. He carried some rocks from the nearby mountain and placed them on the grave:

"Rest now, O good man, and may this grave take its place as part of those sacrificial grounds where the leading lights of our fatherland were massacred. This killing field will be an eternal sign to the coming generation, a reminder of their suffering past . . . It will spur them to lay a more secure basis for their present . . . And then, perhaps, will the blood of their forefathers open up the road to liberation."

CHAPTER 5

HAVING pressed his father's body into this unworthy grave the young man, totally immersed in bitter thought, continued his journey once more and set out now like someone completely possessed. Having lost father, mother, brother and sisters, he was now in terrible fear of losing the woman he loved, as well. But it was still a long way to her village.

He pressed on along the rocky path which was surrounded by chaparral so dense that a thousand men could have been hidden there without showing the slightest sign. He was therefore quite alarmed when he heard a faint voice. Within a few moments the voice became clearer and he realized that someone was calling his name. But who could it be, here in the middle of nowhere? It's true he had comrades, but he had sent them off on missions to various places. Thinking this might be one of them, he put his fingers to his lips and whistled a special signal. The response came from quite nearby, but this seemed very odd. "This can't be one of my comrades," he thought to himself. Just then the name Sarhad struck his ears again and a pair of arms suddenly wrapped around his neck and a man began covering his face with kisses.

"Don't you recognize your own servant?" the man said in Kurdish.

"Msdo, of course I recognize you!" said Sarhad, returning his embrace.

By ethnicity Msdo was a Yezidi[19] Kurd. He had been a shepherd for Sarhad's father, and the two of them had grown up together and always been close friends. When Sarhad had last seen him he had left Msdo a chubby, lively, loyal youngster, but now, lightly armed with a rifle, sword and pistol, he found him in the fullness of manhood. Sarhad was overjoyed to find him, especially since he could provide vital information on what had happened in his absence.

"Ah, how stupid I am Sarhad, I barely recognized you," said Msdo with his characteristic laugh. "As soon as I saw you, I hid in the bushes and trained my rifle on you . . . Just as I was about to fire, I noticed the scar on your forehead, and I said to myself, that is master, and I didn't fire . . . Ah, how you've changed; the devil himself wouldn't recognize you!"

Msdo threw his arms around Sarhad again and began kissing his master.

"You were actually going to kill me, Msdo?" asked Sarhad.

"Ah well, I was after your spear because mine was broken. You know how shameful it is for a Kurd to be without a spear!"

"How did it get broken?"

"I had to fight against some Kurds when they raided our sheep. They took them all. The infidels took your colt, too, Sarhad—that blue one. Ah, if only you could have seen what a beautiful horse he turned out to be! I fed him plenty every day and fattened him up, because I told myself someday you'd come back and live at home again. They stole him and all the sheep."

"Our sheep?"

"Yes, who else's? You know Msdo never owned any. I even took a bullet in my foot, but I hit a few of them, too."

"Where were you off to, limping like that?"

"I was going over that way . . . There was something . . ."

"What?"

"Oh, I get tongue-tied trying to tell you. . . The damned Kurds . . .

My master. . ."

Msdo couldn't finish what he had to say, his eyes filled with tears and he started sobbing like a baby.

"They killed him . . . I already know. But what were you going to do?"

"I was going to bury him. I couldn't leave him like that—he was a good man."

"I already buried him," Sarhad answered sadly. "Tell me, do you know anything about my mother, my sisters, my brother?"

"I know too much; there's no pain I haven't seen. Do you want me to start at the beginning?"

"No, just keep it short. I'll ask the questions and you answer."

"Ask me then."

"When did the Kurds get here?'

"Two nights ago when everyone was asleep they swooped down on the village. Other Kurds raided the other villages. There weren't many of them here, barely a hundred, but ten would have been enough to do the job. What's wrong with the Armenians, master? Why aren't they brave? It's terrible, really terrible. There was a lot of screaming and wailing when they broke down the doors and rushed into the cottages. 'You helpless wretches,' I said to the Armenians, 'You're not women, but men. So you have no swords or guns—fight them off with sticks or stones or kick them if you have to, just drive the dogs away.' But who would pay any attention to me? First the Kurds picked out what they wanted—property or women—and left the rest in the cottages with the old people and the children. They shut them up in their cottages and set fire to them, then they killed the boys."

"Didn't anyone survive?"

"Only those who got word of what was about to happen and were able to escape into the mountains. But most of the villagers didn't believe the Kurds would do anything like that. The *kaimakam*[20] had sent word that everyone should stay put and not worry about anything. He tricked them, the damned liar!"

"And what happened at our home?"

"Your father wasn't home, he had gone to Bashkala. Before he left he told me, 'Msdo, take care of things until I get back.' I was awake and standing on the roof with my rifle when the Kurds got here, but what could I, Msdo, do against such monsters? If I had had just ten men with me I could have kept them off, but I was by myself and I didn't lift a finger because I knew for sure what would happen if I did: no one would be left alive. I was looking for some way to save the family. I thought to myself, 'Whatever's left, to hell with it, let them take it.' So I got your mother, brother and sisters out of the house right away. But I was so stupid, I forgot the baby was still inside in the crib. Your mother cried, 'My baby! My baby!' and ran back toward the cottage. There I was, caught between the tips of two swords and I didn't know which way to go: If I left the girls, the Kurds would get them. I'd better hide them first, I thought, then come back for your mother. So I hid your brother and sisters in a barley field and ran right back for your mother. When I got back I saw the house in flames, but your mother ran inside without paying me or the flames any attention, then the roof collapsed and she never came out again.

Sarhad listened to all this, petrified and as pale as marble. His thin lips quivered in a fever of distress, but there were no tears in his eyes.

"Why did my father go to Bashkala?" he asked in a trembling voice.

"When people found out about the Sheikh's order to kill the *gavours*, they panicked; they didn't know what to do or where to escape to, so your father called together the *danouders*[21] of all the villages. A priest and a *vartabed* joined them, and they all went to Bashkala to ask the *moudour* and the *kaimakam* to send troops to protect the villages from the Sheikh's army. The *moudour* and *kaimakam* put things off until the next day, but by that time the Kurds arrived and they saw their opportunity. The delegation saw that the *kaimakam* had tricked them, and they left with their hopes dashed. Meanwhile, the Kurds found out they had gone to see the *kaimakam*, and they attacked them on the road as they were returning. You saw with your own eyes what they did to them . . ."

"Where are my sisters and brother now? I hope they haven't run into any danger," said Sarhad, fully expecting the worst.

"They're in good hands. I took them to my tribe, and they're with my wife in our own tent. Yes, you didn't know, Sarhad, but I have a wife and child now! And such a beautiful child! Your father—God bless his soul—married me to a good girl and gave me a hundred sheep. He said, 'Msdo, you've served me long enough, go now and live on your own, start a home and be your own master.' But I said to him, I've grown up on the food you fed me, agha, and I'll stay in your home until I die. I'll stay with you and be your oldest son until Sarhad comes back."

On hearing these words Sarhad's heart gave way and he embraced Msdo and kissed his forehead.

"We'll be brothers again, Msdo and we'll never part. But are you sure my brother and sisters will be safe in your tent?

The young Kurd responded with bold self-confidence:

"You know yourself how zealous Yezidis are. Sheikh Jalaleddin with all his bandits could never set foot in Msdo's tent. One Yezidi's guest is the whole tribe's guest, no matter what his nationality, and they'll defend him at the cost of their own blood."

Msdo suddenly stopped talking to listen to something.

"Do you hear that, those voices?" he asked.

"What voices?" asked Sarhad, so distracted he hadn't heard anything.

"It's singing, the song Kurds sing when they're carrying off captives and loot."

"Then let's get going," said Sarhad.

"Yes, let's go," echoed Msdo.

The two of them headed in the direction of the sounds.

CHAPTER 6

A HALF hour later they reached the crest of a mountain from which they could see a caravan moving through the valley. It was too far away to be seen clearly, but it had a distinctly odd and suspicious appearance.

"If we want to head it off we should go this way," said Msdo, indicating a barely visible hunters' trail.

"But we shouldn't be seen," said Sarhad sternly.

"They couldn't see us, even with a thousand eyes. I know these mountains like the back of my hand. Let's go."

The trail was full of precipitous ups and downs but so direct that they soon by-passed the caravan and took cover in bushes to spy on it. Sarhad could see at a glance that it consisted of a large number of Kurdish marauders transporting booty and captives.

"Msdo, if you can, please go to the caravan and find out where the captives are from and where they're being taken. We also need to know what tribe the Kurds belong to and where they plan to stop for the night."

"I'll have all the answers when I get back."

"How are you going to present yourself?"

"However necessary—they can't eat me up! I'll go and greet them and ask them how they are, then the rest will come to me . . ."

"All right, get going then, every moment counts."

Msdo vanished like a ghost and Sarhad now took a closer look at the caravan. It was a motley file of oxen and donkeys pulling carts piled high with all kinds of household goods. Individually or in pairs the captive women, girls and boys were tied to the top of each load, being carried off on the backs of their own families' animals and brutally driven forward by the Kurdish horsemen. To ensure the rapid progress of the caravan the marauders had stuck human heads on the tips of their spears like scarecrows, the heads of the captives' own parents.

Sarhad couldn't look for long at this horrific sight and his head began to swim as the caravan passed before his eyes.

It seemed to him that the world had changed; that the anti-Christ had appeared on earth; that men—created in the image of God—had turned into crazed monsters who sucked the blood of their fellow beings and devoured their flesh. He, too, wished to be a monster like that. He had all the necessary virility but, alas, he was alone and without comrades.

Despair often pushes a man to the extremest forms of reflection. Though Sarhad was good by nature, circumstances had made him evil. He saw a people—his own people—slaughtered like chickens, their houses reduced to rubble, their property plundered, their children carried off into slavery; a people without the slightest means of defending itself.

He knew that these same atrocities had been visited upon them for centuries, yet that they had never once considered defending themselves. He thought, "If people are guided by necessity and make clothing to protect themselves from the elements and fashion weapons to protect themselves from wild animals, how could it not occur to them to defend themselves, as well, from beasts in human form?" So thinking, Sarhad had concluded that a people who didn't grasp what life demands and failed to understand that it shared the earth and had to deal with men, not angels, such a people was itself at fault . . .

Sarhad had wandered far and wide in the world and seen many different peoples and places but had never once encountered anyone he considered truly good. He therefore held a dim view of his fellow human beings and regarded all men as bandits—with the qualification that one bandit crudely ravages with a sword, another does so with his wits, another through trade, another beneath the banner of philanthropy and culture, etc.

Sarhad had his own way of expressing these ideas. He would say, "Banditry appears in many different guises among people, and often it comes in colorful, attractive packaging, but if you tear away the wrapping you'll find nothing but banditry inside."

Sarhad was himself a terrible and bloody bandit. If he had been born in another country and grown up in a different environment he might have become a very different person, a different sort of bandit, since the kind of bandit one becomes depends on what kind of society one is born into. The bandit stands as an awful protest against the unjust organization of society. In the highlands of Armenia two peoples faced off against each other: on one side the Armenians, reduced to the nadir of subjugation, and on the other side the Mohammedans, who had arrived at the zenith of barbarism. If, in this situation, the oppressed were to raise a protest against their violent domination, this could plainly take no other form than Sarhad's criminal character.

But truly remarkable was the fact that there were so few Sarhads. His whole band consisted of just twelve brave men whom he called "The Apostleship of Bandits." To further understand this matter would require a long and detailed examination, but we have to set that aside, for Msdo has just reappeared. Let's see what he has to say:

"I got all the answers you wanted," he told Sarhad.

"Tell me point by point as I ask you. How many riders are there?"

"At least fifty. I took a count."

"From which tribe?"

"The Hardoshis."[22]

"Where are their loot and captives from?"

"From around Shadakh."[23]

"Where are they going with them?"

"To Soma."[24]

"Where do they plan to stop for the night?"

"Near Khana-Sor, in the lowlands of Haspidan."

Sarhad paused for a moment to figure something on his fingers, then asked:

"When do you think they'll get to the Sakhgal-Toutan[25] Pass, Msdo?"

"Shortly before sunset."

"Right. Now tell me, how long do you think it would take you to get to Bizhingerd? Are you familiar with it?"

Msdo took a look at the sun.

"Right at noon," he answered.

"Good. Did you ever notice a chapel in a little valley close to Bizhingerd?"

"Yes, there are two chapels there, one of them is in ruins. Which one do you mean?"

"The one in ruins."

"I know it well. I spent the night there once after I stole a horse. It's a perfect hide-out."

Sarhad had just one more question for Msdo:

"What kind of animal sounds can you make?"

"Lots of them. I can bark like a dog, crow like a rooster, bray like a donkey, howl like a wolf, bleat like a sheep, meow like a cat. I can go pee-poo like a hoopoe. What others would you like? I can do a lot more."

"The last one will do. Now listen, go straight to the ruined chapel; but before you get there, there's a hill . . ."

"With a *hole-rock*[26] at the top," added Msdo.

"Yes. You'll stand at that *hole-rock* and make the sound of the hoopoe three times. You'll be answered with the same sound. Then you'll make a different sound. You'll hoot twice like an owl. A man will show up. You'll tell him that they have to be ready at the Sakhgal-Toutan Pass just before sunset."

"What if he asks who sent me?"

"Give him my name."

"But he probably won't believe me."

"Then show him this," said Sarhad, taking his ring off his finger and handing it to Msdo.

"And if he asks what it's all about?"

"Just tell him the whole story of what you saw—the caravan and the captives. Tell him the caravan has to be stopped just when it's inside the pass. All the loot and captives have to be freed from the Kurds."

"I understand. How many men will there be?"

"Twelve."

"Who are they?"

"My comrades."

"Fine, twelve men against fifty will do in the Sakhgal-Toutan Pass," observed Msdo. "But I'll make the thirteenth and thirteen is an unlucky number."[27]

"If you count me, that will make fourteen. Fourteen isn't unlucky," said Sarhad.

"Four of us will be enough to block the pass, and even the devil himself couldn't get out of it," observed Msdo. "What a perfect place you picked, Master. But where will you be?"

"I'll secretly follow the caravan until it reaches the pass. But tell me, isn't your foot going to bother you? It's a long way to Bizhingerd."

"No, it won't bother me. The damned bullet went through the flesh, but it didn't touch the bone. I dressed it with *mahlam*[28] and bandaged it up."

"How many days has it been"

"Three days. But Msdo has seen a lot of wounds like this; it won't be a problem."

"All right then, get going."

Sarhad and Msdo parted. One set out on the road to the chapel ruins, the other left the beaten track to continue shadowing the caravan from the uplands.

CHAPTER 7

BY now the reader is quite familiar with Sarhad, but the time has come to get better acquainted with the other members of his band as well. Though he was their commander he addressed them all as 'brother', and for good reason. All of them were truly united by the closest of fraternal bonds. They met together at various times and places and rarely exceeded a dozen men. Among them were Sassountsis, Zeytountsis, Shadakhtsis, Diarbekirtsis, a priest from among the Kurdish speaking Armenians of Kharpert, and a teacher. The teacher had been a member of a philanthropic organization in Bolis and it had sent him eastward to bring learning and education to the various Armenian villages of Van. But he had been forced to join Sarhad's band in the troubled times of the Russo-Turkish War after his school was invaded by Kurds and he was severely beaten in front of his class. Some of his pupils were also abducted in that incident, but they were later released.

Sarhad's band looked and acted like Kurds. They avoided the name "Armenian", but not because it was offensive to them. On the contrary, they cherished their Armenian identity. But going by that name didn't well serve either their activities or their purposes. In their wandering existence Sarhad and his band fell into repeated clashes with the Kurds and were always settling scores with various Mohammedan tribes and therefore couldn't let it be known that they were Armenian. Otherwise their enemies would take their vengeance out on pitiful, defenseless Armenians who weren't even aware of their existence.

Sarhad was in the Diarbekir area with his band when he first got word of the wild agitation that had taken hold among the Kurds and the formation of Jalaleddin's terrible army, as well as of Sheikh Ibadullah's hellish meeting.[29] Sarhad immediately rushed toward Aghbak with his men. Two motives drew him back to the homeland he had long since put out of his mind: First, the fact that Aghbak was in the direct path of the Kurdish invasion and would bear the brunt of the worst marauding and his corresponding wish to extend a helping hand to his brethren there; secondly, and most important, there was someone there who held a very special place in his heart.

All the bitter utterances that had come out of Sarhad's mouth as he went searching through the devastation of his homeland, all the terrible words he had let loose over his dying father's head—these were all the sighs of a heart brimming with despair, graveside laments expressed in the funereal silence that hung over his native land. For he had reached the breaking point, the point of maddening rage on finding Aghbak far from what he had wished it to be. He was fully conscious of the evil in which he had been caught, horrified by the blood on his own hands, though he had only used them to defend sufferers and never to spill the blood of innocents. Yet it hurt his pride to see that despite all his potential he had been reduced to the role of a mere bandit chief, whereas, in reality, he had what it took to command an entire army in the task of liberating his homeland once and for all from the reign of bandits . . .

Sarhad set off alone for the city of Van after having sent his comrades off to different parts of Aghbak with instructions to give the various villages there whatever help they could until he arrived. In Van he presented himself to the Pasha and informed him of the danger the Armenians of Aghbak were under. He asked the Pasha's permission to form a people's militia in Aghbak to defend the peasants from the coming invasion of the Kurds and *bashibozouks*. "The government itself has everything necessary in hand," he was told and his request was denied.

Knowing full well how meaningless such statements were Sarhad left Van empty-handed. It was at this point that we first encountered him, sad and alone and with a heart full of despair, making his way toward Aghbak along the Khoshap Valley road.

But his determination was undiminished, and on reaching Aghbak he made yet another attempt to implement his plan. He called on a number village notables—various pastors, *vartabeds* and *danouders*—and urged them to lend their support to the creation of a popular militia to defend the peasants from the impending invasion. Even though Jalaleddin's invasion had still not started, there were increasing signs of Kurdish barbarism in every quarter. In support of his argument he pointed out to them the example set by the neighboring Assyrians of Jolamerik. They had armed themselves so effectively that not a single Kurd had dared set foot on their land, and even the government was powerless to disarm them, because, given its inability to provide them with protection, the Assyrians had asserted their right to self-defense. Sarhad cited many other similar cases to arouse and encourage them; he exhorted and harangued them and went on and on in every way he could think of to try to win them over to the idea . . . But the notables only looked at him as if he were a moron or a madman, something that was even more repugnant to him than the Pasha's deceit had been. This experience convinced him once and for all that the Armenians were themselves responsible for their abject subjugation and that they themselves had prepared the way for all the hardships they were suffering.

From the moment he left his comrades he had no way of knowing their whereabouts or what they were up to. They had parted only with the understanding that they would meet next at the "chapel ruins" on a certain date. But the unexpected sighting of the caravan forced him to send his loyal servant Msdo in his place to the chapel ruins and through him direct his band to the Sakhgal-Toutan Pass where they would make an attempt to rescue the captives.

Msdo's mission wasn't fruitless and at the appointed hour Sarhad's entire band stood ready at the pass. Seeing all his comrades assembled there Sarhad embraced each one then stood back to address them:

"I'm so happy to find you all in one piece, at least physically, but I know you come here with aching hearts because of all the barbarous destruction and slaughter you've seen. But today we have a superb opportunity to put our bravery into practice. That's why I called you here. The fourteen of us will have to deal with more than fifty wild Hardoshis."

"Msdo told us all about it," said the priest, now known as Dali-Baba.[30] "With this cross I'll pronounce a splendid benediction over the Hardoshis' heads," he said, holding up his sword.

"This truly is a wonderful opportunity for us. We'll have a fine go at the Hardoshis down in the pass," said the animated school teacher, now known as Kitab-Dalisih.[31]

"That's right, if you're going to challenge Hardoshis, it's best to do it in tight places like that. The devils are real fire breathers," said Sassountsi Haro, now called "Sassoun-Ayus" which means "The Sassoun Bear."

"We're wasting our time with this foolish talk. The Hardoshis aren't going to be pushovers," observed Zeitountsi Nerso, known as "Zeitoun-Kayas", that is, "The Zeitoun Rock."

"Yes, time is slipping away so let's focus on our mission," said Sarhad. "You all know how brave the Hardoshis are. It's stupid to think they're going to be child's play. All we have going for us is place and position.

That's why I chose the pass. Lie hidden behind the rocks until the caravan is completely inside the pass. We'll divide up into two groups. Seven men will block the entrance to the pass and seven will block the exit. I'll signal the attack with a falcon's cry. Try your best to limit the bloodshed and speak only in the Ravandi dialect, because the Ravands and Hardoshis are enemies. They have to believe we're Ravands. If they surrender I'll state the terms to them. And remember, your attacks shouldn't always be from the same place or side. Change your positions often so they think there's more of us than there are and immediately shoot any of them who try to escape so they don't get away and carry word to the others."

The Sakhgal-Toutan Pass is one of those formidable passes such as one frequently encounters in the mountains of Armenia. Its rocky walls tower up on right and left leaving only the narrowest passage through which pack animals can pass in single file.

Sarhad and his men found the weary caravan strung out in this manner from one end of the pass to the other, advancing very slowly. Sarhad postponed any action until the sun was down and darkness set in. But it was a moonlit night. He took six men with him and went to block the exit to the pass, and left six men with Dali-Baba to go and block the entrance. The caravan was in between, filling the narrow gorge as if caught inside a gigantic tunnel with both ends shut.

Suddenly the sharp and penetrating cry of a falcon about to strike its prey rang out over the gorge.

Rifle fire exploded all around. A wail of confusion and alarm rose up from the gorge. The Hardoshis began darting all over like beasts gone mad, but every move they made was met with the roar of gunfire. The lion had fallen into an iron trap.

It is in moments of danger that the Kurd shows the sublimest qualities of his nature. He turns into a veritable dragon, fully prepared to gulp down boulders or mountains if he must. The sheer, jagged walls of the gorge seemed as nothing to the fierce Hardoshis. They charged up them like tigers, struggling to come face to face with the enemy. But nature got the better of them and they finally lost their footing and slipped down to the bottom of the gorge again.

The mad outcry from the Hardoshis, the wailing and moaning of the captives, the gunfire exploding from right and left all filled the gorge with a terrible harmony. The battle went on and on with bestial obstinacy. The Hardoshis were determined to fight to their very last breath. But a falcon cry sounded three times, the signal from Sarhad to yield no quarter, and a thundering barrage of bullets hailed down into the gorge.

The clear moonlit night considerably aided the battle and our brave ones aimed well. They were able to target only the Kurds and leave the captives unharmed.

After another hour of desperate fighting a voice was heard from deep in the gorge: "We give up!" Sarhad stepped out on a rock far above the vanquished Hardoshis and spoke:

"You should have given up a long time ago, but you chose instead to be stubborn and keep fighting. Because of that most of your men have died needlessly. It's not that bad, though, because that's a warrior's fate. I compliment you on your daring. Listen now to my conditons: You'll all stay in the gorge but give up your booty, your prisoners, and all the animals carrying them. We won't take your weapons or horses; you'll need them. Just give up what you stole, stay put in the gorge until daybreak, then you're free to go where you want. Agreed?"

"Agreed!" came a voice from the gorge.

"Now—release the prisoners and the booty."

Within a few hours the gorge was vacated; only about twenty Hardoshis remained.

"Dali-Baba," said Sarhad, "Take four men with you and drive the caravan toward Salmast. You'll cross the Persian frontier by sunrise and in Salmast these poor people will find safety with the local Armenians, because that's where all the Aghbaktsis found refuge when they fled from Jalaleddin's army. Salmast is in Persian territory and no Kurds from Turkey are allowed across the border. And listen, don't give the slightest sign that you're Armenian. The captives must never find out our true identity. When you and your comrades return from Persia you'll find us in the valley of Irtz in the cave you're familiar with. Meanwhile, I'll keep that scum in the gorge until you're well on your way and I'll let them go just before sunrise."

"Damned if I ever gave a sermon that long when I was a priest!" said a distinctly exasperated Dali-Baba. "Good Lord, why go into such fine detail about everything, I'm not a novice in this work."

"As our forefathers said, listen to what others say but keep your own counsel," said Sarhad with a laugh. "Now get on your way and the Lord be with you."

The caravan moved off toward Salmast with all the haste of a man just freed from mortal danger. The heartfelt blessings of gratitude from the liberated multitude could be heard in the silence of the night, their tearful eyes raised toward their saviors . . .

A few days later word spread throughout Aghbak that some Hardoshis had carried off an enormous haul of booty and captives from the Shadakh area, and that in the Sakhgal-Toutan Pass a band of Ravands had descended on them and taken it all away and disappeared to parts unknown. There wasn't a word mentioned in all of this about Sarhad or his band. Because incidents of Kurds stealing booty and captives from each other were so commonplace the news made no great impression on anyone, and it was out of the question to suspect Armenians, for they were seen as incapable of carrying out such acts. Sarhad's band had clearly succeeded in passing themselves off as Ravands.

CHAPTER 8

THERE wasn't one Armenian left in the entire province of Aghbak. Twenty-four villages lay devastated and empty.[32] Some of their inhabitants had been killed, some had been captured, and the rest had fled to the border towns of Salmast and Soma in Persia where they found refuge with the local Armenians.

So sudden and unexpected had Jalaleddin's invasion been that those who escaped with their lives did so only narrowly. As for home and hearth, goods and animals, all had been abandoned to the enemy.

The invasion was like some horrible and never ending flood, one that advances then recedes, then comes back again and again to strike with the renewed fury of its whirlpools. Thus, having left nothing but ruin and desolation in his wake, Jalaleddin left Aghbak and set out for the battle of Bayazid with a cavalry of only five thousand men. But by the time he reached the region of Bayazid, Kurds from far and wide had heard of his exploits and flocked from great distances to join their leader's army and bring it up to full strength, and thus it was that the ravaging flood came back time after time and swept over the land.

Jalaleddin in his dual role as sheikh and general was the man who had been given responsibility for leading the Kurds to the battlefield. But there was another sheikh who enjoyed far greater power over the Kurds than any other, a man who had stirred them up into a perfect frenzy, and that was Sheikh Ibadullah.[33] He was the supreme spiritual leader of all Kurdistan and, while never moving from his spot, exercised tremendous influence over all the Kurdish leaders—the *derebeys,* the *gatis*, and the *mouftis*[34]—by means of his religious proclamations. This sworn enemy of all Christians had given the nod for the most terrible atrocities to be committed against them and called for no mercy to be shown in the process.

The Kurdish and other Mohammedan tribes take up arms in war time for two basic reasons: blind fanaticism, on the one hand, and lust for plunder, on the other. For two passions, the spiritual and the material, are at play here. The first is satisfied by slaughtering non-believers; the second by looting everything they own. This accounted for the slow progress of Jalaleddin's army as it made its way toward Bayazid. On one side was the imperative to gather loot, but on the other was the necessity of disposing of it before moving on, since it wasn't possible to carry it all to the battlefield. It was therefore necessary for Jalaleddin's fighters periodically to detach themselves from the army and carry their harvest back to their various homes, then catch up with the army once more to continue on. Thus did Jalaleddin scour everything in his path as he worked his way to Bayazid.

Nevertheless, it can't simply be denied that there are also many kind and decent Kurds, individuals who would never be a party to such evil. Omar Agha was one of these—a Kurd who owned a wealth of herds and flocks and was the chieftain of his little tribe. Not only had Omar Agha refused to join in Jalaleddin's campaign, but on learning of his barbarous plans immediately went to the monastery of St. Bartholomew to warn its abbot, Eliazar, about the terrible calamity the Armenians of Aghbak would be under in only a few days. He advised Abbot Eliazar to take advantage of the monastery's unbreachable fastness, gather the wealth of all the surrounding Armenian villages there, and from this sacred fortress make a stand against the enemy. He promised to join forces with the the abbot and made good on his word, because he himself was afraid of Jalaleddin and dreaded the vengeance he might exact on him for not taking part in his campaign. So he brought all his goods and possessions to the monastery and was prepared, together with all his men, to join the Armenians in taking a stand against the enemy.

Abbot Eliazar, having complete confidence in his old friend, accepted his advice and arranged for all the inhabitants, goods and animals of the surrounding villages to be gathered into the monastery.

St. Bartholomew's[35] is one of those ancient monasteries that have endured since the days of The Illuminator.[36] For all of sixteen hundred years, contending with the elements as well as the attacks of barbarians, this monastery stood as a gigantic monument to the architectural mastery of the devout Armenians. It had witnessed many atrocities: the cruelties of the fire worshipping Persians, the barbarities of the Arabs and the Mongols. Its spendid walls bore countless reminders of the many times it had been destroyed and then rebuilt through the dedication of the Armenians.

The monastery stands in a commanding position on the brow of a steep hill, its foundations resting on artificial earthworks added to the top of the hill to further increase its elevation. It is surrounded on three sides by a deep valley with one of the upper tributaries of the Euphrates flowing through it. This tributary is commonly known as "Monastery River". The remaining side of the hill is joined to the flank of a mountain with an Armenian village on it. This village is less than a hundred paces away from the monastery and belongs to it. It is accordingly known as "Monastery Village."

The monastery is surrounded by high walls and towers. Aside from its magnificent sanctuary it houses an array of cells for monks, numerous workrooms for daily tasks, and shelters for all the livestock. As soon as word of Jalaleddin's invasion reached the district all the populace from the surrounding villages crowded into the monastery for protection and soon filled every available space. Their animals were driven to "Monastery Village" and their valuables were hidden away in the numerous secret storage chambers of the monastery.

The broad, level margins of "Monastery River", now thickly carpeted with grass and glittering with yellow flowers at the start of spring, was the grazing ground for the monastery's animals. Everyone was therefore totally shocked one morning to look down and see it covered with tents. Since Kurdish shepherds had no right to encroach on the monastery, let alone pitch tents on its land, these must have been the self-invited guests whose arrival had been so feared. Everyone panicked, and from every corner of the monastery they started driving its sheep, cows, and draught animals to "Monastery Village". Their shock was further heightened when a shepherd came to Abbot Eliazar and reported that, indeed, the tents in the valley belonged to Jalaleddin and that his army had spent the previous night there.

Abbot Eliazar was a gigantic man. Though he was quite old and his hearing wasn't what it used to be, he had, due to his close dealings with the Kurds over a period of many years, become "half Kurdish", as they say; which means that he had developed a fearless and manly disposition. He was sitting in his little cell together with Omar Agha when the shepherd arrived to report Jalaleddin's presence in the valley but, unlike the faint-hearted who wither at the slightest news of danger, he remained calm. On receiving the report the two men rose and went out to look. They walked to the eastern wall of the monastery and stood silently for many minutes with their telescopes trained on the tents pitched along the river below.

"That's him all right. And the old bandit's got himself a good sized following, too," said Omar-Agha with noticeable anxiety.

"What do you think we should do?" asked the abbot with equal anxiety.

"The monastery is well fortified and defensible. All we can do is gather the villagers inside and shut the gates."

"Exactly what I was thinking. I hid a good cache of rifles and gun powder away in the cellars a long time ago, just in case. I'll have them passed out to the men who know how to use them. I know quite a number of them who are good at it."

"And my men will be arriving at any moment to join us, too. But whatever you need to do, make it quick. We don't have a moment to lose," said Omar-Agha.

Abbot Eliazar left Omar-Agha standing at the monastery wall peering down on Jalaleddin's camp through his telescope as he himself went off to make all the necessary preparations.

Several different religious traditions exist among the Kurds. Omar-Agha and Jalaleddin belonged to sects that were opposed to each other. Confessional differences have the same impact and produce the same kind of divisions among Kurds as ethnic differences do, especially in times when contact between them has been severed due to polarising conditions. It was on this basis that Omar-Agha's tribe took exception to the tribes who followed Jalaleddin.

But the abbot's plan met with stiff resistance from the people inside. No one went along with him. "If we lift a finger we'll all be killed," they protested. "If we touch so much as a hair on their heads, they'll burn us alive and massacre our families. No, we won't resist. Let them come and take what they want, anything to spare our children . . ."

"They'll come just the same and take away everything you own. How can you believe they'll spare anyone? . . ." said the *vartabed*, his eyes welling with tears. "Listen to me, this holy monastery will protect us if only we rely on it. We have plenty of men and Omar Agha and his men will be with us, too."

But no one wished to hear any of that. "Impossible!" they all shouted. "If you're serious about saving us, then go with some priests and *danouders* and talk to the Sheikh. Kiss his feet and beg him. Tell him we'll give him whatever he wants as long as he lets us live."

The valiant *vartabed* persisted, nevertheless. He exhorted and scolded the faint-hearted, servile crowd, but to no avail, and they held their ground. He was finally forced to pull together a delegation and go to parley with the Sheikh.

At this point Omar Agha came and said to him:

"I knew it would come to this, but it won't do you any good to see the Sheikh. You'll be taken prisoner, and there's a good chance they'll kill you."

"I'm going, I have no choice. If they kill me, so be it. The people won't give me any peace . . ."

"If that's your decision there's no reason for me to stay any longer" said Omar Agha.

"And I'm not urging you to stay. Go, and the Lord be with you. But before you leave I'll ask just one favor of you. Take this key. There are two chests that belong to the monastery stored in the same place we hid your belongings. They contain our monastery's holiest articles. Please take them with you so they're not looted. You've shown more dedication to us than any Christian."

"Rest assured I'll take care of them," replied Omar Agha. "But one of my men has to go with you and keep an eye out to see if they take you prisoner. That way I'll know what happened."

The two men embraced and Abbot Eliazar set off for the Sheikh's camp without any expectation of ever returning.

Omar-Agha's men arrived on the scene with around thirty extra horses. They loaded up the the two chests the abbot had asked Omar-Agha to take with him as well as their own property that they had brought for safekeeping just a few days before. When Omar-Agha was finally ready to go, the gate keeper opened the secret doors in the wall, and, with a heart full of sorrow, the noble Kurd bowed down and kissed the holy altar, then left.

Abbot Eliazar went to the Sheikh's camp, never to return again . . .

A few hours later the Kurds began entering "Monastery Village" one wave after another and drove the livestock out. They then emptied all the cottages of whatever goods they wanted, loaded them onto the animals and set them forth on the road. When they had finished with the village, they went to the monastery where all the wealth of the district had been stored and started to carry it out. The wailing and moaning of their pathetic victims had no effect at all on the callous hearts of these marauders . . . The least resistance was met with the immediate punishment of sword or pistol.

And so—this was the atrocious event that was unfolding while Sarhad and his band were enroute to St. Bartholomew's monastery the night after their courageous feat in the Sakhgal-Toutan Pass.

But what could young Sarhad expect to find in that half-destroyed and deserted monastery?

CHAPTER 9

IT WAS a dark and starless night. It seemed the earth and sky were fused together into a single mass of blackness. There was silence everywhere, except for a harsh nocturnal wind that presaged a storm. Lightning flashed from time to time over the faraway mountains, and the distant sound of thunder tapered off into ever smaller rumblings as it passed through the night-enshrouded mountains.

In this eerie nocturnal setting several shadows were stirring about in the dark like wandering ghosts. They came together into a small group and seemed to confer, then divided up again and one by one started making their way toward Monastery Village.

The village was dark and still and like a vast cemetery every sign of motion or life had ceased. The only light to be seen came from the enormous hulk of the monastery sitting atop the hill surrounded by a deep, dark abyss. The only sound to break the prevailing silence was that of the river with its infuriated murmuring and moaning down below.

If at that hour one had entered the structure the light was coming from, the following is the tragic spectacle that would have greeted one's eyes: A once beautiful sanctuary totally stripped of all its majestic features, nothing but emptiness beneath its magnificent dome—no crosses, nor books, nor pictures, nor great candles—nothing! The sacred altar, splattered with blood, was like a scene from a slaugherhouse.

Some horses were tied up on one side eating hay. On the other side was a group of Kurds sitting around a fire. Wooden furnishings from the monastery—chairs, lecterns, doors—were continually being broken to bits and fed to the fire. Several spits and bronze cauldrons were set on the fire and by now glowing so hot they could barely be distinguished from the embers themselves. Nearby a group of men with their legs shackled together were sprawled on the bare floor awaiting their fate with horror. Next to them was a jumbled pile of sacred objects from the church. The leader of the Kurds stood up and went over to them.

"Tell me what else you've got hidden away, infidels!" he demanded. "Speak up! Don't hold back anything or you'll be killed like dogs. See those glowing spits? They're being prepared for *you*."

"We bow down to your feet, sir. Please have mercy on us and don't kill us !" said the shackled men. "That's all there was, there's nothing more. If that's not so, then may God blind our eyes and throw our souls in hell."

"You're lying, you damned dogs!" roared the Kurd. "There used to be a whole king's ransom in this monastery. What became of it?"

"Sir, may we be the ground you walk on. Please have pity on us, don't kill us . . . May God turn us to dust us if we lied about anything. That's all there was. They took everything. Nothing is left. You know very well how many times we've been robbed in the past few days. . . If there had been an ocean, it would have gone dry; if there had been a mountain, it would have melted away . . ."

At that, the interrogator wheeled around and called to his men:

"Bring the spits! These damned infidels won't come out with the truth until they feel them."

Several Kurds took hold of the prisoners and began stripping them down, while others brought the spits from the fire.

"Begin! But burn them in the form of a cross. They love crosses," ordered the leader. The executioners began laying the glowing spits against the bare chests and other body parts of the prisoners, and they sizzled against the living flesh. The first set of spits was then placed back in the fire and another set was taken out to continue the hellish ordeal. The victims were gasping and moaning in pain.

"Stop! Just kill us all at once and be done with it! For the love of God, get it over with!" they begged. But despite their unceasing, pathetic clamor the process went on and on until the point that what they were saying had turned unintelligible and only their deep gasping could be heard . . .

"Enough!" ordered the leader.

He then turned to one of the victims who hadn't been tortured yet, a priest.

"We saved you for last so that your torture would be the finest," he said sarcastically. "Do you see that red-hot bronze bowl in the fire that looks like a crown? I'm going to put it on your head since you're a priest."

The priest answered with religious sentiment:

"My Lord accepted a crown of thorns, and as His humble servant I'll gladly accept the bronze bowl . . . But remember one thing, sir: There's a God above, the Lord of us all, who sees everything you're doing here. He won't let you go unpunished if you spill innocent blood. Why torture us for no good reason? My brothers told you the truth, there's nothing left in our monastery to give away. Whatever there was, we gave you. We opened all the secret storerooms for you. But even so, you had to cruelly and heartlessly go on and despoil St. Bartholomew's grave, thinking you'd find some treasure buried there. Whatever there was, Jalaleddin took it away, and Kurds came ten times over after that . . . You're just the last ones . . ."

"You're lying, you sneaky dog!" roared the monster. "Bring the bowl!" he ordered.

One of the men took the glowing bowl out of the fire with tongs and brought it over. The priest, this servant of God's altar, waited with a martyr's patience for the barbarous act to be executed. He was still and quiet, except for the slight movement of his lips as he mutely muttered a prayer . . . The Kurds uncovered his hoary head and were about to cap him with the red-hot bowl when suddenly pistol shots rang out and the whole sanctuary was filled with smoke.

Panic reigned as several Kurds were struck and fell to the floor, while others were powerfully seized and bound. All this transpired in just a few moments in a deep silence. All that could be heard was the voice of the priest:

"For the love of God, don't kill them. Let them do what they want with us. If you hurt them they'll massacre all the Armenians."

Though the pitiful clergyman didn't know who these suddenly appearing saviors were, he was afraid that any such killing inside an Armenian church would bring the vengeance of the Kurds down upon all Armenians, despite the fact that it had never crossed any Kurd's mind that the cowardly Armenians were capable of such brazen acts . . .

Except for their eyes, the intruders' faces were completely covered. Their clothing and speech were Kurdish. There were just a few of them, but they had burst in so suddenly that they had managed to kill several Kurds outright who were the closest targets. Then they grabbed hold of the others, bound them up tightly and led them out, though it wasn't clear where they were being taken. In just a quarter of an hour two of the intruders returned and set the priest and his half-dead brothers free.

"There's still plenty of nighttime left," they said to the priest and the others. "By sunrise you'll be able to reach the Persian border and there you'll be safe. We have enough horses for all of you. Gather together everything the Kurds were going to take and be ready to mount and get out of here with it as soon as possible."

"But there's hardly a breath of life left in my brothers," said the priest.

"A couple of our comrades will accompany you," they answered.

The priest bowed down and clasped his rescuers' feet.

"There's no need for that. Just be prepared to leave as soon as you can."

"But I have to know who rescued us," said the priest.

"No! You shouldn't know," they answered.

"What nationality are you?"

"You shouldn't know that, either."

Within a short time the rescuers had packed the saddlebags and loaded them onto the Kurds' horses tethered inside the sanctuary. Then they set the victims of the red-hot spits on horseback and sent them off.

Before the priest had mounted, he again addressed the strangers:

"At least let me give you my blessing."

"That's not necessary either," one of the men said. "Just answer some questions for me."

"Go ahead and ask."

"Is no one left in Monastery Village?"

"No one."

"What happened to the villagers?"

"Some of them fled to Persia, some were killed, and the others were captured."

"Did you know someone in Monastery Village named H . . . who was the *danouder*?"

"I knew him. I myself am the priest for the village."

"Do you know what became of his family?'

"The *danouder* was killed. His sons weren't home and they escaped. But the Kurds took his daughter away."

These last words struck Sarhad's heart like lightning. After several moments of stunned silence, he asked:

"If you could, just tell me what direction they went with her and what tribe they belonged to, I'd be very grateful."

"As to where they took her, I couldn't say. But they were Cholakh-Ahmet's men, of the Shikag tribe."

"That will do. You can go now," said Sarhad in conclusion.

The priest and his comrades, accompanied to the road by two of their rescuers, left to begin their journey to the Persian border. Twelve of the band remained in the sanctuary, and at this point one of them pulled the mask away from his face evidently to breathe more freely, and the firelight fell on the deathly pallor of Sarhad's face.

While his comrades were cheerily carving up a huge boar and sticking the pieces on their ramrods to roast over the fire for dinner, he sat near the fire trying to find a bit of relief from all his inner turmoil. But Msdo kept a careful eye on his master as if trying his best to read his troubled expression.

Poor Sarhad! There had remained but one consolation in his life, and now that, too, had been taken away. Here in the environs of the monastery he had hoped to find that lovely being to whom his heart belonged, the only love he had found in a hateful world. But she was nowhere to be found. She had been taken away under terrible circumstances . . .

Love isn't the only feeling a freedom fighter bears in his heart toward women. There is another feeling which we have various inadequate words for—jealousy or ardor or zeal—a feeling that nevertheless remains inexpressible in a few dry words. It is the passion that kept the Greeks fighting beneath the walls of Troy for ten long years, the drive to honor the sacredness of women.

Sarhad was suffering not only because he had lost his beloved, but even more because she had ended up in unclean hands . . . Yet how many innocent women were there who found themselves in exactly the same situation, and who was there to worry about them? Their parents, perhaps? A poor father or mother—if they had been left alive? But did the nation care—the Armenian people? No, for that would require a hellenistic zeal.

As he passed beneath the gloomy arches of the monastery, old, old wounds were opened in Sarhad's heart, for this sanctuary was tied to his feelings with the deepest of memories. Here he had spent the most precious years of his youth, placed under the care and close supervision of prayerful monks to study what religion and the holy scriptures have to offer, doctrines that extinguish spiritual vitality and dull the mind . . . And near these same monastery walls an angelic beauty had ecstatically brought him back to life and revived in him a heart that had perished in monastic disease. With her redemptive hands she had pulled him from the darkness and placed him once more in the broad daylight of the world.

All the while he sat near the fire totally lost in these doleful memories his comrades went about producing a lavish dinner reminiscent of Homeric heroes. Large cups of wine were being passed from hand to hand and the meat was being torn off the spits still bloody. No one wanted to disturb Sarhad in his melancholy revery and everyone just let him alone as they fell to eating. But then Dali-Baba stood up to make a toast and Sarhad looked up to see what he had to say. Facing the altar of the church Dali-Baba raised his brimming cup of wine and pronounced the following hermetic toast:

"O fathers! O forefathers! I drink from this cup, but not to you. If instead of all these monasteries that you filled our homeland with you had built fortresses; if instead of exhausting our wealth on the purchase of holy crosses and sacred vessels you had bought weapons; if instead of filling our churches with clouds of sweet smelling incense you had burned gunpowder, our homeland would already be free and the Kurds wouldn't be here raiding our villages, killing our children, ravaging our women . . . Our country's destruction began here in these monasteries, for it was in them that our courage and daring were extinguished. Since the moment Drtad exhanged his sword and crown for the cross and disappeared into Maniah cave to practice asceticism, these monasteries committed us to slavery . . . O ancient gods of the Armenians! O Anahid! O Vahakn and Haik! It's to *your* sacred memory that I drink from this cup. *You*, come and save us!"

Thus over a cup of wine that held the power of cheer did this fearsome character give vent to all his bitterness—a man who at one time had been a priest but now found himself in the shoes of an outlaw. When he was finished and sat back down, another member of the band followed suit and stood to deliver a toast of his own. Known to his brothers as Kitab-Dalisih, he had been a school teacher at one time, but now found himself a member of Sarhad's bloody band. He spoke as follows:

"O Letters and Learning, I drink from this cup but not to you, because you denied us what life and reality demand and filled our minds instead with vain and abstract illusions. You didn't show us what we needed to survive and live safe, stable lives. Instead you inculcated us with dark superstitions and sealed our eyes to the light and the truth. You turned us into corpses in which every exalted human impulse had died.

You forged the chains of our enslavement and taught us to bear the shameful, crushing yoke of oppression. O Letters and Learning! We owe our present suffering to you! You deprived us of sound mind and thought, and in denying us true knowledge you deprived us of life itself . . . Therefore, curses be upon our press which, with all its obfuscation, has filled our hearts, our minds, and our souls with darkness . . . And long live those writers who inspire a new spirit in us, who replenish our exhausted energies, who teach us what life really requires and prepare us for a full humanity with all its attributes."

In this vein spoke the man they called "Crazy From Books", a man who had been reduced to foolishness by too much reading but was now a new man.

Sarhad took all of this in and listened in melancholy assent. Their words came as a relief to him and lifted him for a moment out of his personal crisis to focus again on the general suffering of all. A lover's particular love gave way to the love for an entire victimized people, a people whose daughters and wives had fallen into an identical captivity. He therefore reacted coolly to Msdo when he approached and said in a low voice:

"Master, don't torment yourself. Msdo has a nose as keen as a dog's. If *she* is in the depths of the sea, he'll find her. If *she* is up in the sky, he will bring her down."

CHAPTER 10

IT WAS near the end of July. After ill-fated Bayazid was encircled by Kurds and *bashibozouks*; after it was destroyed and looted and its poor inhabitants were put to the sword or carried off into captivity, it fell into Russian hands again. Suleyman Pasha had pulled back. Jalaleddin's horde had dispersed and were on their way home with a rich load of spoils. The entire province of Pakrevand and historic Vagharshagerd had been emptied of their Armenian population, the refugees from Alashgerd were begging in the streets of Yerevan district, and the ruins they had left behind were in cinders and still smoking.

The afterglow of sunset still lit up the mountain summits.

A lone young man was walking slowly along a narrow mountain road, singing a dark and melancholy melody. His steps seemed indecisive, as if he had taken this route against his better judgement and doubted that it would lead him to the goal he had set for himself at the cost of great self-sacrifice. He suddenly heard a voice ring out behind him:

"Hey you, out of my way!"

The young traveler stopped singing. He lifted his rifle from his shoulder and turned around and saw a rider approaching.

"Go on by," he answered.

The rider came closer and greeted him:

"May all be well with you! Where are you going?" he asked.

"Thanks be to God, I'm fine. I'm one of Jafar-Bek's shepherds. Our camp is nearby. One of our females got lost and I'm looking for her. But godspeed to you, where are you headed?"

"I'm delivering a letter to the Sheikh's army," the rider responded.

"Who from?"

"From Suleyman Pasha. Things aren't going well in Kars. The Pasha summoned us and told us, 'Whoever can get this message to the Sheikh in two days will receive a promotion and a robe of honor. I went up and bowed my head to him. 'May I be the dust beneath your feet, I'll deliver it. My Arabian steed flies like a bird,' I said to him. He patted me on the back and said, 'Good for you!' and handed me the message."

"Where is the Sheikh now?" asked the young traveler.

"They told me he was camped nearby in Ghanli-Darah. How is it you didn't know?"

"How would a highland shepherd hear about such things? Every day they come and go and you can't tell what's going on."

"By the way, do you have a light? My flint's all used up," said the rider.

"I'll get some," said the young traveler. He took some flint and tinder out of his pocket and when he had struck up a flame the rider bent down with his pipe to light it, allowing the young traveler to get a clear glimpse of his face. The rider thanked the young man and rode off puffing on his pipe, but he had gone no more than ten paces when a rifle shot roared out behind him and he fell from his saddle. One of his feet remained stuck in the stirrup, however, and the horse pulled his body to the side of the road and began running up and down in a terrible panic dragging it over the rocks. Finally the saddle slipped all the way down to its belly, and only then did the horse calm down. By this time every bone in the rider's body had been broken.

The assassin approached. After securing the horse he searched through the rider's clothing for the message to Sheikh Jalaleddin. He found it and slipped it into his shirt then dragged the man's body to the nearest ravine and dropped it in. He came back to the horse, straightened out its saddle, then mounted and sped off toward Ghanli-Darah and Sheikh Jalaleddin's camp.

He reached the camp at sunset. The message he carried was rolled up into a cylinder and sealed with a paper band as is the custom in the East.

Before entering the camp he took it out of his shirt and stuck it in his turban so that it would show prominently as he approached.

"Who are you?" asked a guard at the entrance to the camp.

"A messenger," replied the bearer, then boldy spurred his horse on to the Sheikh's tent without awaiting the guard's response.

That man was Msdo.

CHAPTER 11

AFTER their horrific battle with the Kurds inside St. Bartholomew's sanctuary, Sarhad and his men spent the night there. The next morning just before daybreak they were making preparations to leave when they suddenly discovered that Msdo was missing. Sarhad's men were all shocked, because Msdo was cunning and bold enough to do anything, and they were convinced that he had run off to betray them.

"I don't question Msdo's loyalty, precisely because he's a Kurd. A Kurd isn't false, whether to friends or enemies; he doesn't change his colors," said Sarhad.

After missing for three whole days, Msdo reappeared.

"I found her!" These were his first words, as he threw his arms around Sarhad's neck.

"Who?" asked Sarhad.

"Your beloved, Asli!"

Sarhad fell into a kind of intoxication.

In full detail Msdo recounted to Sarhad his encounter with the Pasha's messenger; how he had killed him, then stolen the message he was carrying, passed himself off as the real messenger, delivered the letter to the Sheikh's camp, and finally found Asli among the captive women.

"You're absolutely sure she's there?" Sarhad asked with great excitement.

"Of course. I saw her with my own eyes and talked to her," said Msdo happily.

"And she recognized you?"

"As soon as she saw me she was going to run to me, but I signalled her not to, and she checked herself."

"But how did you manage to find her?"

Msdo then recounted how the Sheikh had ordered him to stay over for one day to give him enough time to consult with his advisors and compose a response, and he was provided with dinner and quarters near the Sheikh's tent. It was in this situation that Msdo encountered "one of his own", a Yezidi he had previously known and who now served as a personal attendant to the Sheikh and prepared his pipe for him. The man invited Msdo into his own quarters as an honored guest and offered him the hospitality due a co-religionist and compatriot. Since they were old friends Msdo trusted him and asked if he could show him the captive women, and that was how he had found Asli. At that point Msdo leveled with his friend that his true purpose in coming to Jalaleddin's camp was to set Asli free. His friend promised to smuggle her out of her quarters and hand her over to anyone Msdo designated.

Sarhad listened in total amazement, hardly believing his own ears. "Do you really think your friend will keep his promise?" he asked.

"A Yezidi isn't quick to make promises, but when he does he keeps them," said Msdo with noticeable pride. He then added that he knew a secret from the man's life that proved his credibility:

"A few years ago the Sheikh ordered his brother to be killed, so he became an attendant to the Sheikh to avenge his brother's murder. The Sheikh has no idea who he is or what his religion is."

"Given what you say he can be trusted," said Sarhad, convinced at last. "But how can he get Asli out of the camp?"

"She'll be dressed as a boy and just walk out of the camp on her own. Msdo isn't stupid; he's made sure of everything. We have to go to a little dale near the camp tonight and be ready to meet her. There's an old pear tree there, and that's where we'll meet her."

After a few moments of reflection, Sarhad asked, "How many other captive women are there?"

"The Sheikh has kept a hundred or so women and girls for himself. There are several tents full of them near his tent."

"Do the other men have captives too?"

"All of them have several. Many of them were bought up by Ushnetsi[37] Jews to sell them back to the Armenians. They're very cheap to buy; one girl goes for a silver mechitya (20 kopecks of one rouble)."

Sarhad's somewhat brightened expression now clouded over again, and acute pain reigned once more in his heart . . .

This conversation between Msdo and his master took place in privacy at a far off spot which was next to a spring gushing from a cleft in a mountain rock. Sarhad's comrades were sleeping in the grass in the distance, resting from the previous night's battle. Sarhad went and woke them up to tell them the news that Msdo had brought and announce that he had to go to Jalaleddin's camp.

"Not without us," they all answered.

CHAPTER 12

GHANLI-DARAH means 'The Valley of Blood', a name well earned from the countless bloody deeds that have taken place there. This valley is the sole domain of brigands who use it as a haven, and no caravan or traveler has ever safely ventured there. Following the tragic events at Bayazid, Sheikh Jalaleddin and his army had likewise taken refuge in Ghanli-Darah after quitting the field of battle.

One of the upper branches of the Tigris, called Nahel by the locals, flows through this valley and divides the districts of Aghbak and Jolamerik from each other. It was in a level area on the banks of this river one night that hundreds of little fires were twinkling, with Kurdish fighters sitting around them smoking, laughing, singing.

From time to time they checked the kettles of food cooking over the fires and turned over chunks of meat roasting over the coals. Demented forms of entertainment gave further evidence of the general light-hearted mood that prevailed on every side. The only light came from the fires. All the tents were dark but one, and that was Jalaleddin's tent.

Far from the camp in a narrow valley that branched off from Ghanli-Darah, the sound of drums and Kurdish *zournas*[38] could be heard playing the "Janiman" melody. A group of horsemen was riding through the area at the time and the wild music caught their attention.

"There's something strange going on," whispered one of the riders to the man next to him.

"Just what I was thinking."

"We'd better take a closer look."

"I agree, let's go."

The riders spurred their horses toward the sound of the festivities, but their way was soon lost in thickets and they were forced to dismount. They left their horses in a comrade's care and proceeded on foot. Within a few minutes they reached the top of a hill and looked down to see the following abhorrent spectacle:

It was a scene the like of which Dionysus with all his bacchic immorality could not have imagined. On one side were drums and *zournas* playing music; on the other side was the dance, taking the form we call the *Yalli* and known as *Zvant* by the Kurds. The dancers were women, their hands joined together and moving around in a large, chainlike circle. For torchlight long poles were stuck in the ground in the center of the circle with bits of oil soaked clothing flaming atop them and casting a purple light over the ashen faces of the dancing women. Men sat beneath the torches, looking with hellish excitement at the chain of naked women moving constantly by.

That these pitiful women had been forced to participate in this perverted dance was obvious. They had been brought to the point of raging madness by the shame and dishonor to which they had been subjected. Their eyes flamed angrily, their lips trembled in a fever of distress, and grotesque twitches could be seen in their faces. Many were so weak they couldn't put up with their suffering any longer and fell to the ground unconscious. All of this that should have alarmed a humane conscience, that should have softened and filled any heart, no matter how hardened, with pity and a sense of honor toward the fairer and weaker sex, all of this on the contrary only further provoked the wildest instincts and bestial excitement of their captors.

The dance went on with all the hellishness of a forced performance. The line of naked women kept moving around to the sound of the drums. The men sitting in the center were singing, clapping, roaring and shouting. From time to time, one of these heroes threw his handkerchief over the woman of his choice and dragged her off to the bushes, the pairing of an angel and a devil.

Of all the cruelties of mankind none is more terrible than this, that complete innocence be sacrificed to unchecked force. Such extreme cruelty is unique to humankind, for even wild animals show greater decency than this in their relations with females.

The group of men hidden at the top of the hill looked down with disgust at this shameless torchlit entertainment transpiring in the dark of night. The reader knows who they were.

"We have to attack," said Sarhad

"But there are so many of the devils."

"So what? We have to die someday; maybe this is the place," responded Sarhad.

"But you came for Asli. What about her?" asked Dali-Baba.

"Every one of those women needs our help as much as she does," said the noble youth, setting aside personal love to defend the honor of all victimized women.

"We have to make a lightening attack and put the torches out first thing. It has to be dark if we're going to get anything done," said Dali-Baba.

"Look, the moon just disappeared and it's totally dark now," noted Kitab-Dalisih.

"But use only swords. Jalaleddin's army is in the area and gunfire will attract their attention."

Down below in the dale the Kurds felt perfectly at ease. They had come to the spot armed only with their swords, each man with his chosen victim in tow.

Msdo couldn't bear what was going on. It was clear that Sarhad had completely forgotten about rescuing Asli. Instead, he was on the verge of launching a bloody engagement that he could barely expect to survive. Msdo didn't know what to do. Should he stay to fight and possibly die beside Sarhad? That was his first, high-minded inclination. On the other hand Asli was languishing in the Sheikh's large harem, an angelic girl who had been Sarhad's love since childhood. Without a word to Sarhad Msdo slipped away to head for the Sheikh's camp.

The attack began with lightning speed after Msdo had gone. The torches were immediately extinguished. Darkness and terror reigned in the dale as the horrible killing began.

Hand to hand fighting is a truly horrible affair, especially when confined to close quarters in the middle of the night. In a life and death battle of that kind the steel of a sword wreaks terrible havoc on the human body. Under the threat of death, a living man struggles to produce death.

The fight went on with bestial stubbornness for yet another two hours. In the heat of battle one comrade struck another with his sword. Desperate and painful cries merged with the clash of weapons. Both the killers and the killed were drenched in blood as more and more bodies fell to the ground and were trampled as the fight continued.

Light fell on the dale once more. The moon emerged from the ashen clouds as if to glimpse some lovely sight, but in its light was suddenly revealed a heart-wrenching scene instead. Soon understanding that this fight was for them and their freedom, the enslaved women had thrown themselves into the battle like mad Furies. A woman's ferocity in exacting revenge for a sense of personal violation is truly an awesome thing. Shedding all femininity in such moments, she becomes an angel of death and will thrust her hand into the very heart of the person who has trampeled on her honor. And so, these women who only a few hours ago had been reduced by brute force to the lowest form of degradation, now, having heard the sounds of their own freedom, snatched the weapons from the hands of their prone captors and started to finish them off. Honor battled against brutal passions; angels fought against devils . . .

The moon was lost behind the clouds again, and the black curtain of night descended once more to cover the entire scene in darkness.

Not far from the western shores of Lake Van at the foot of Mt. Sipan a group nomads' tents could be seen standing along the verdant banks of a little stream, the modesty of their appearance indicating that their inhabitants weren't members of the more prosperous Kurdish tribes but rather quite humble shepherds. These were the tents of Yezidis, Kurds who were more persecuted even than the Armenians, and here in this isolated mountain spot they had sought shelter from the brunt of war for themselves and their flocks.

It was a week after the horrific carnage in Ghanli-Darah, and in one of these tents that looked exactly like all the others lay a sick young man with sunken eyes and a face as pale as death, apparently suffering from very serious wounds. He could barely draw a breath or turn from one side to the other. This was Sarhad. A young girl sat near his pillow, her eyes welling with tears and an agonized expression on her face. This was Asli whom Msdo had succeeded in rescuing during the events at Ghanli-Darah. To Sarhad's right and left two other girls were sitting like angels of sadness and also weeping. These were his sisters. In a corner of the tent, hunched over with his hands over his eyes, was his little brother. And outside, Msdo himself stood sobbing near the entrance to his tent.

Sarhad was in his last moments.

Only three wounded comrades had survived the battle of Ghanli-Darah. All the others had fallen. Also lost in the battle were many of those valiant women who had with their blood sanctified their struggle against violent depredation . . .

The wounded lion opened his eyes for the last time, looked at Asli, looked at his sisters and his brother, then closed his eyes . . . "Akh" was the last word he uttered.

"You've died in my tent, O brave, and now it's up to me to avenge your death. I will . . ." said Msdo with a sigh, cradling Sarhad's head in his arms.

END NOTES

CHAPTER 1 NOTES:

1. cushion — *taghik*
2. prayer beads — *taspek*
3. sheikh — Among the Kurds, the spiritual leader of a community or tribe.
4. *agha* — a man of high social standing; lord, landlord, master.
5. *kashkoul* — Raffi's note: A vessel carried by dervishes, made either of a coconut shell or a melon-shaped seashell. [translator's note: the kashkoul is the traditional "begging bowl" of the dervishes. It is elaborately embossed and carried on a fine double chain of silver.]
6. prophet of Arabia — Mohammed
7. *gavours* — non-Muslim minorities, infidels.
8. *halal* — Raffi's note: *halal* means those things that are not forbidden.
9. *talakh* — Raffi's note: *Talakh* means luck or spousal union, which is considered destroyed when a Kurd breaks a vow. The Kurd says, 'May my wife be *haram* (forbidden) to me if I break my vow," for the spousal bond is considered as sacred to the Kurd as chivalry is to the freedom fighter.

CHAPTER 2 NOTES

10. Bashkala — Raffi's note: The citadel town for Aghbak district.
11. *moudour* — the chief civilian authority of a town.
12. Heidaran — a Kurdish tribe.
13. Sipan mountain — A volcanic mountain north of Lake Van, the second highest peak in the Armenian Highland after Mount Ararat.
14. Bilbasts — The Shikags, Ravands and Bilbasts are Kurdish tribes.
15. *Fuleen* — lit. peasant, disparaging Kurdish reference to Armenians.
16. Harkis — Raffi's note: This is a wild tribe of Kurds who live all the way from the upper reaches of the Tigris to Mosul.

CHAPTER 3 NOTES

17. Drtad's Cross — Raffi's note: a constellation.

CHAPTER 4

18. *vartabed* — a celibate priest who specializes in scholarship and teaching.

CHAPTER 5 NOTES

19. Yezidi — a distinctive group of Kurds who never accepted Islam and whose religious traditions, including synchretistic influences from Christianity and Islam, can be traced back to Zoroastrianism.
20. *kaimakam* — the governor of a province.

21. *danouder* — (pronounced, dawn-oo-dare)the elective headman and innkeeper of a village, usually the head of the most prosperous household.

CHAPTER 6 NOTES

22. Hardoshis — Raffi's Note: A half-civilized tribe that never settles anywhere.
23. Shadakh — Raffi's Note: a district of Vaspuragan* [for which, see entry below - tr.] Shadakh is due south of Lake Van and west of Bashkala. In present-day Turkey it is known as 'Chatak'. tr.).

    Vaspuragan — A key Armenian province containing the city of Van, Lake Van and the adjoining regions; this constituted the heartland of Western Armenia. Bordering in the east on the Persian district of Salmast, where Raffi was born, the Aghbak region lies in the mountainous easternmost portion of Vaspuragan.
24. Soma — Raffi's Note: a district of Urmia province in Persia.
25. Sakhgal-Toutan — an unofficial name for the pass, "beard-catcher" in Turkish.
26. *hole-rock — dzag kar.* This term is rendered literally from the Armenian. Tufa formations are widespread throughout Armenia, many with holes in them. Some of these holes have been either made or shaped by human beings over the centuries and may have mystical or astronomic significance.
27. unlucky number — *nas*. Raffi's Note: *Nas* means bad or unlucky. The number 13 is regarded as *nas* by Mohammedans. When they count, on reaching the number 13 they pause for a moment and say 'not 13.'
28. *mahlam* — a medicine derived from wild cherry.

CHAPTER 7 NOTES

29. "hellish meeting" — This is Raffi's expression for the following situation:

    On returning from a pilgrimage to Mecca just before the outbreak of the war, Sheikh Ibadullah was invited to meet with Sultan Hamid in Constantinople. At this meeting he was presented with gifts and given important guidance and support for his future activities. This honor from the Sultan was the prelude to the subsequent atrocities committed against the Armenians and other Christian minorities in eastern Anatolia.
30. Dali-Baba — Raffi's note: Dali-Baba means "renegade father", a name well suited to his unconventional character who had traded in his Christian timidity for the vengefulness of the Old Testament.
31. Kitab-Dalisih — Raffi's note: Kitab-Dalisih means "crazy from books."

CHAPTER 8 NOTES

32. empty — Note taken from Raffi's report, *Holy War and the Situation of Christians in Asia Minor* [*Mshag,* June 1877]: "Of the twenty-four villages mentioned, nineteen were Armenian and five Assyrian. The Armenian villages were: Monastery Village, Bizhingerd, Baplasar, Pars, Sorader, Yeringyani, Chukh, Yeresan, Zeynis, Keredj, Haspidan, Kharadon, Malkavil, Bas, Arak, Alas, Badgan, Lashgod and Garbesh.The Assyrian villages were:

Adess, Ardji, Hoghi, Bavess Manglavin. It's impossible to ascertain the exact number of total inhabitants, but these villages were very densely populated."

33. Sheikh Ibadullah — A detailed treatment of this historic figure can be found in chapter 4 of *A Modern History of The Kurds* by David McDowall, pp. 53 - 59 [I. B. Tauris, 2000].

34. *mouftis* — the *derebeys,* the *gatis,* and the *mouftis* — *Derebey* means literally 'valley lord'. The *derebeys* were feudal Kurdish lords who, from the 18th century on, became semi-independent of Ottoman rule. *Gatis* and *mouftis* are Islamic judges who decide cases of Koranic law, the *gatis* being state appointed figures whose judgements are enforced by the state, and the *mouftis* whose judgments are issued as *fatwas* whose validity rests on their personal authority and credibility.

35. St. Bartholomew's — Despite repeated attempts of the Cilician See of the Armenian Church to have this structure recognized as a cultural treasure and included in the UNESCO list of protected historic sites, it today lies in ruin, with only its exposed foundations and a few remaining blocks from its walls resting on them.

36. The Illuminator — St. Gregory The Illuminator, the founder of the Armenian Church, early 4th century.

CHAPTER 9 — NO NOTES

CHAPTER 10 NO NOTES

CHAPTER 11 NOTES

37. Ushnetsi — From Ushnuk. Ushnuk is a city in Persia near the southwestern corner of Lake Urmia; also known as Oshnovieh.

CHAPTER 12

38. *zournas* — The *zourna* is a double-reed folk instrument, related to the oboe, used in Persia and adjoining regions. It's body is of carved fruit wood and it has a flaring "bell" similar to that of a trumpet. It has a loud, raucous sound and is traditionally used on festive occasions together with vigorous drumming.

GOMIDAS INSTITUTE
RAFFI
THE FOOL
RAFFI
JALALEDDIN
RAFFI
THE GOLDEN ROOSTER
RAFFI
TAJKAHAYK
RAFFI
THE FIVE MELIKDOMS OF KARABAGH (1600-1827)

www.ingramcontent.com/pod-product-compliance
Lightning Source LLC
LaVergne TN
LVHW050943080826
845145LV00004B/1393

* 9 7 8 1 9 0 9 3 8 2 5 7 2 *